Samsung S4 Tricks and Traps

Master Your Device in Less Than 1 Hour

Disclaimer

No part of this eBook can be transmitted or reproduced in any form including print, electronic, photocopying, scanning, mechanical or recording without prior written permission from the author.

All information, ideas and guidelines presented here are for educational purposes only.

While the author has taken utmost efforts to ensure the accuracy of the written content, all readers are advised to follow information mentioned herein at their own risk. The author cannot be held responsible for any personal or commercial damage caused by misinterpretation of information. All readers are encouraged to seek professional advice when needed.

Quick View of the Guide

Samsung is the market leader of the telecom industry and rightly so, due to the incredible gadgets it comes out with. This time it has made a powerful entry by launching the successor of it S series, with the ***Samsung S4***. So if you have already bought the device or you are looking to buy it, this guide will give you tips and tricks that will allow you to get the most out of your device.

However, in order to do that, this guide will take you through the basic features and specifications, along with 100 tips and tricks including:

- Secret shortcuts that will allow you to maneuver easily from one application to other.
- Applications to allow privacy control
- Applications that will allow you to carry out office work anywhere you go.
- Health, fitness applications.
- How to make the best use out of the inbuilt applications.
- Other useful tricks, tips and shortcuts.

The more you know about your Smartphone, the more you will enjoy using it. So, keep on reading to master your Samsung S4.

Contents

Samsung S4 Tips Tricks and Traps

Tip#1: Ensure Your Safety

Samsung has come up with a great way of keeping its users safe, as much as a Smartphone without Artificial intelligence can. It is called the 'Safety Assistance'. Safety assistance can be enabled by going to the 'My device' in the settings menu.

You will find Safety Assistance in 'My device'. By enabling Safety Assistance, people who lead a riskier life or live in dangerous areas, can alert specific numbers on their predetermined emergency list. When you sense you are in danger, all you need to do is press and hold the volume, up and down key.

By pressing and holding down the volume key, your device will send alert messages to all those people on your emergency list, along with your exact location and a snap shot from your rear facing camera and one from the front facing camera. You will be required to enter these numbers when you enable the safety assistance. This is one great feature to ensure the safety of its users and hats off to the people down at Samsung who care so much about the safety of their users.

Tip#2: Air View

This is an application that allows the user a glimpse into what gadgets will look like in 5 to 10 years and as always Samsung is one to bring a future technology to its users before its time. You can enable 'Air View', by going into the settings or simply using the notification panel.

Just by hovering your finger over controls and keys, you can access your messages, pictures in the galleries, camera and email and so on. This feature allows you a peek into the folders so that you can get a preview of the contents without having to completely access the application. For example if you want to check Facebook, you hover over the Facebook app and a little popup window will let you see inside the app without opening it completely, so that as soon as you move your finger, the pop up window disappears. It saves a lot of your time and is one of the best features for those people who constantly like to check their emails, messages and notifications.

Tip#3: Your Samsung S4, a Remote Control!

If you've had it with fighting over the remote with your spouse, siblings, and other family members, your Samsung S4 can become a savior for your nerves and a great way to irritate friends and puzzle family members.

With your S4, you can sync any remote controlled appliance or gadget with your phone and use it as a remote. This is possible using 'The WatchON' application, which allows your S4 to become your own personal remote control and a TV guide. Once you have any electrical gadget synced to your phone, all you need to do is go to the application screen and click the 'WatchOn' application, move into the settings and go to the remote control in the notification panel. You can sync any kind of device such as your home theatre, DVD player and so on.

Tip#4: In Call Clarity Optimization

This feature is an answer to the prayers of all Smartphone users. How many times have we had to call a person repeatedly in order to get a better reception during calls? Using this new feature, Samsung allows us to enhance our call quality during the call!

The in call sound equalizer allows you to increase and decrease the call volume, by tapping the touch buttons during the calls. You can increase extra volume as well, which maximizes the level even if your phone is at its maximum volume, along with softening or sharpening the voice quality, also using the in call touch options.

The best bit is the 'Noise reduction' option, which allows you to filter the surrounding noise in the call, best used when you are in a busy place such as a mall or on the street. This feature allows you to hear the voice on the other end of the phone as clearly as if they were sitting right next to you.

Tip#5: Pop-up Keyboard

As much as Smartphone manufacturers are trying to replace laptops with Smartphone, they have not been able to make multitasking in a Smartphone easy. In fact multitasking can get irritating to say the least, due to the time it wastes going back and forth from one app to another.

The good news is that S4 has eased multitasking a great deal and has introduced several features that allow a user to multitask effortlessly. It is the pop up keyboard offered by S4 that allows you to use the keyboard no wonder what app you are using, with the Multi Window application.

Tip#6: Blocking Mode

Although most of us like to feel connected with our friends and family wherever in the world they might be, but sometimes all we get are unnecessary notifications and messages from sales persons announcing sales. Unexpected notifications not only eat into our battery life but our actual lives as well. When our phones ring at the wrong time it can have dire consequences, which is why Samsung has brought this amazing feature to the S4 phones.

Using the blocking mode, you can block all notifications as long as you want, just by tapping the on screen button in the notification panel. When you are ready to receive notifications, you can switch the blocking mode off just by tapping the same button. You can also add an allowed number or two so that your device will filter all calls except from these allowed numbers, so you don't have to worry about missing a call from office or home, or any important person.

Tip #7: Command your photos and videos

Keeping with the theme, the phone from the future, Samsung S4 allows you to control more features using your voice, than ever before. Now you can snap photos and record videos just by commanding your phone to do so.

To do so, you will have to enable the voice feature by clicking the icon with the microphone on it in the camera's settings. Once you have enabled the voice feature, all you have to do is say' Shoot' or 'cheese' if you want to snap a picture. If you want to record a video, simply say 'record video' and your command will be done.

Tip #8: Screen shot

A lot of times the best way to share an article, a picture or anything on your screen is by snapping a screen shot of it and immediately sending it to your friends and family. It is one of the easiest options of sharing with friends anything you find interesting due to the convenience and ease of carrying it out.

Capturing a screen shot is super easy using S4, press the home button and the power button at the same time to snap a screen shot and you will see the screen flash if a screen shot has been captured. You will find the screen shot in the gallery.

Tip # 9: Smart Stay

A lot of the times, the screen switches off while you are going through pictures or watching a video. If you have to change the display witch off time every time you are want to use your cell phone for longer and it is simply wasting precious battery juice. An easier option, provided in the S4 is the smart stay feature.

Enabling the smart stay feature allows will keep your screen on as long as you are looking at it. You can enable Smart Stay just by clicking on the option by expanding the options by pressing the toggle keys in the notification panel.

Tip # 10: Get More Out of the Camera App

The camera app in the new S4 has all kinds of tricks to help you capture amazing pictures for sharing with your friends and uploading on your social media profiles. Your best bet is trying out all the features so that you get used to using them and thus can make the best use out of them.

By pressing the mode button, you can see and use all the different modes that are included in the S4. You can also take a look at all the features by pressing the icon on top of the screen that has four boxes in it. With each mode, you can see a description of what the mode does for your pictures. As a result, you can create gifs or drama shots as easily as 123.

Tip # 11: Multi Windows

There are a lot of apps that you would like to run simultaneously, or maybe run one in the background while using another. For this purpose solely, S4 brings to you the Multi Window option. However what use is having a list of applications that you don't like to use simultaneously on the multi window. This is why, Multi Window feature allows you to edit and customize the list of applications that you can use simultaneously by going to the Multi window option and enabling it first of all. Then Going to the edit button you can add or remove applications from the side bar by dragging and dropping applications into and out of it.

Tip # 12: Set limits on Wi-Fi Timer

If you do not have an unlimited data plan than probably you have a hard time controlling and staying within the limit of your data plan. However using this new feature in the S4, you can easily and conveniently control your internet usage.

Don't pay additional charges and instead use the allotted time well by setting a limit on your data usage along with reminders that let you know how much you have used and how much is left. Simply go to the settings menu and then select the Connections setting. From the Connections settings, click on the Wi-Fi settings, go to the advanced menu and then you will see the 'Wi-Fi Timer'. Select the Wi-Fi timer, and adjust the starting and ending time of your Wi-Fi connection as per your own preferences.

Tip # 13: Take Watching Videos to the Next Level

Now you don't have to watch your videos on the fixed small screen or the standard screen options, because Samsung S4 brings you video watching options that will allow you to take the experience to the next level. For starters, you can enlarge or zoom your screen, just by using the pinch-to-zoom feature. You can zoom more than ever, you can brighten, and you can increase or decrease the volume, using the scroll buttons on the right and left. The scroll buttons will appear on the screen by touching the right or left side of the screen.

Tip # 13: Easily Access the Camera

There are a lot of times when accessing the camera in a hurry can take so long that, that the moment you want to capture is lost. It might also be that you don't want someone to get into your Smartphone, but in order to capture a shot you are required to grant them access to your device no matter how much you are against it.

For this reason, Samsung S4 brings you this new feature to allow easy access to the camera app. In the new S4, you can access the camera app from the lock screen. To enable accessing camera from the lock screen, all you need to do is to go to the settings menu. In the settings menu, go to 'my device', from this select the Lock screen, and go into the 'Lock screen widgets'. From amongst the widgets, select camera. Launch the camera by swiping to the left on the lock screen.

Tip # 14: Modify Lock Screen Message

Let your Lock Screen reflect your personality using this new feature in the S4. You can add a message and display it in your favorite font and color. In order to activate this feature, go to the settings and u can activate this option by going to the settings menu. In the settings menu, go to 'my device', from this select the Lock screen, and go into the 'Lock screen widgets'.

In the Lock Screen Widgets, go to the 'Edit personal information'. In this menu, you can select a message, font and colors as well, or you can go to the lock screen and tap the message line and then hold it, while dragging it down. Doing so will display a pencil icon using which you can change the message and add a quote that you like or your pet sentence, or anything that you like.

Tip # 15: Smart Scroll or Hypnotic Glance?

The new Smart Scroll option in S4, allows you the greatest of ease when browsing internet, reading books or doing anything at all. Using Smart Scroll you can navigate the screen using your glance. By looking up or flicking your wrist in an upward motion, you can move the screen up and by moving your glance down or moving your wrist in a downward motion, you can move the screen down.

Tip # 16: Dual Video Call

This amazing feature allows you to share your view, literally, with a person you are on the phone with. So you can make calls using front facing camera and the rear facing cameras per your preference. You can also make video calls using ChatOn, the free built in video chatting app in S4.

Tip # 17: Eraser

This is an amazing feature in the Samsung S4, which is nothing short of an answered prayer for all photo lovers. This feature allows you to erase any component of a picture that you don't like, such as an object, a person or anything that is ruining a perfect shot.

Tip # 18: Sound and Shot

Now you can capture sound with a pic, so that you can capture the very essence of a shot that you find perfect. Every time you look at the picture you will hear the sound clip playing along in the background, allowing you to refresh your memories far more clearly now.

Tip # 19: Optimize Sound Quality

Sometimes you find yourself unable to hear your videos or audios clearly, even when playing them at full volume, through your headphones. This can be pretty disappointing, however with the new S4, there is a way out. With the new 'Adapt Sound Function', you can optimize the sound quality of any video without having to keep on increasing the volume.

Samsung has developed this feature keeping in mind the differences in the hearing ability of the right and left ear. In order to optimize sound quality, go to settings and then select 'my device', from this menu select 'Sound'. In the sound menu, choose 'adapt sound' to activate this feature. You need to have your headphones connected for this feature to work.

When you select this feature, you will be able to hear beeps in your ears. You will be then taken through a small test that will help this feature optimize the sound especially for your ears.

Tip # 20: Save Battery Juice

One of the most popular and frequent complaints of any Smartphone user, is their phone's draining batteries. In order to help maximize battery life, Samsung offers its users, in its new device S4, the option to choose and operate on the 'power saving mode', in order to make the battery last for longer durations of time. In order to maximize the battery power, go to the settings menu and select 'My Device', from here, go to 'Power Saver Mode'. In the power Saver Mode, you can customize which applications you want to run all times, how frequently should your device kill apps, and many such options according to your preference.

Tip # 21: Free Cloud Storage

Get free cloud storage when you join Dropbox immediately. However if you are an S4 user, you get a staggering 50 GB of cloud storage absolutely free of cost for duration of 24 months, to use as you will. Sync and set Dropbox to automatically upload all your pictures and videos to your account so that you have a handy backup of your pictures and videos. Send links to your photos and videos to your family and friends so that they can view those precious moments that you chose to capture using your S4.

Tip # 22: Customize Home Screen

Many S4 users claim that their home screen is very intimidating and it takes a lot of time for them to get used to using the device and even then, the device can seem pretty daunting every once in a while. However you can customize your home screen according to your preference and your ease making it easier on your eyes. You can also make it reflect your personality by using colors of your choice along with wallpaper that speaks out to you. In order to customize your home screen go to the 'Settings' menu and select 'My Device'. In the 'My Device' menu, select 'Home Screen Mode', and select the mode you prefer in the menu.

Tip # 23: Translate Text

One of the handiest skills today in this era of globalization is the ability to speak multiple languages. However for those people who have a hard time getting hang of languages, S4 brings a very easy alternate. The S Translator allows you to translate any text to English or any other language simply by speaking the sentence you want translated, into your device and it will interpret the text and display it in English for you.

Tip # 24: Trace-to-type

Trace to type is an easier and more convenient method for inputting text in your S4. Even though touch screens are easy to use, they can still slow you down if you are working on your office documents. Remember the typing speed in the old keyboard phones, now you can match the same speed with your S4 using the trace to type option on your touch keyboard.

To enable trace to type, select your keyboard and tap on the 'gear' icon on the bottom left side of the keyboard. When the drop down menu opens up, select 'Predictive Text', and select 'Continuous Input' as well. Selecting these options will allow you to type by sliding from one alphabet or character to another without lifting your finger from the keyboard to allow continuous input into your device. Lift your finger for adding space to your text.

Tip # 25: S4, an Ideal Weight loss Companion

Samsung comes with pre-installed S Health software that is the ideal companion for anyone setting off on a weight loss journey. It allows you to keep track of your daily calories by adding every meal, snack and morsel to this application which will then calculate your daily calories for you. Along with your calories, this app allows you to calculate your daily calories burned by adding your daily workout to it. The best part although is the pedometer present in the device, which calculates your daily steps for you, and adds it up to give you an accurate idea of how many calories you burn throughout the day. There can hardly be a more helpful application, as it takes all the guesswork out of losing weight for you.

Tip # 26: Lock screen animation

Everyone wants a little sun shine in their life, but a lot of it can get tiresome. Same is the case with the Samsung S4 Lock screen animation. The sunshine animation can get pretty boring after just a little while, which is why Samsung brings you the option to change the lock screen animation unlike ever before. You can select one of the animations provided in the phone or download one that you like. Go to the settings and you can activate this option by going to the settings menu. In the settings menu, go to 'my device', from this select the Lock screen, and then go through the animation options and select one you like.

Tip # 27: Add widgets to your lock screen

Never before has Samsung provided this option to its users. Now you can add an array of widgets to your lock screen for your convenience. Previously we saw how to add the camera widget and now let's look at what other widgets are available to an S4 user. In order to activate this feature, go to the settings and u can activate this option by going to the settings menu. In the settings menu, go to 'my device', from this select the Lock screen, and go into the 'Lock screen widgets'.

Once you are in the Lock Screen Widgets, you can go through all the different widgets available and select the one which will be most beneficial to you. You can add emails, messages, Facebook, Twitter, Speaker, Videos, Mp3 player and all those applications that you use most and want to access easily.

Tip # 28: Enable Glove Mode

To increase sensitivity of your touch phone, enable glove mode which will allow you to use your device even when your fingers are covered, in colder weather. To enable glove mode, go to "my Settings' and select 'My Device'. In the 'My Device' menu, go to 'Display' and select 'High touch sensitivity', in the menu on your screen.

Tip # 29: Get Faster Response from the Home Button

What many users don't know is that, the lag you get when you press the home button is built in, to give you time to re-press the button to launch S Voice. In order to access home Screen quicker when pressing the Home Key, disable S voice, so that your device doesn't lag by giving you the time to press the key again.

In order to disable S voice, go to the application by double pressing the home key. Press the menu key to go into settings. Uncheck the option, "Open via the Home key", to stop the lag.

Tip # 30: Wi-Fi Direct

If you still use Bluetooth to transfer files from your cell to other cells, you are in for a surprise. Wi-Fi Direct is the present and the future of file transfers. Using this feature found in Samsung S4, you can directly send files to anyone using Wi-Fi direct without having to connect to a network or pair.

Tip # 31: How to customize the LED indicator

The purpose behind placing the LED indicator is to indicate that you have notifications. However how do you know what notification is the flashing light indicating? Is it a Facebook notification, a Twitter notification, an email notification, a message notification, Whatsapp notification, Viber notification, Skype notification etc. If you were somehow able to distinguish each notification from the other, it could save a lot of time, not having to check each and every notification on your device.

Well, that is what your S4 allows you to do, color code your notifications so that you know which notification needs urgent attention and which notification can wait. To enable LED Indicator and change settings, go to "My Settings' and select 'My Device'. In the 'My Device' menu, go to LED Indicator and check the box to enable the indicator.

Now go to Whatsapp settings by opening the application and using the menu soft key to bring front the settings menu. Once you see the menu, under the notifications settings, you can customize the color of your LED indicator to any color you prefer. Similarly go to settings for Facebook app, Twitter app, Viber app, Skype app and under notifications panel, customize the color of your LED indicator as per your preference. Now every time the LED light flashes, you would know what your phone is trying to tell you.

Tip # 32: Customize call response

If you are not a fan of the call answering and ending options, you have the option to change these settings to suit your preference, so that you no longer fumble each time your phone rings. To change these settings, simply go to "My Settings' and select 'My Device'. In the 'My Device' menu, go to 'Call' and select Answering or Ending Calls. In this menu you can customize to answer your phone using the keys on your device instead of using your touch keys. Another great option is to activate S voice, using which you can answer your calls just by saying 'Answer' loudly, and reject them by saying "reject".

Tip # 33: Use Your S4 to Control your Game Consoles

IS there anything you can't use your S4 for, apart from cooking your food and taking care of your chores? You can use your S4 to control your USB drives and your Xbox 360 as well. You would require a USB cable although to carry out these tasks. Using your S4, you can gain access to the files inside your USB and your Xbox 360, and copy, or delete any file you want. This is an excellent option for copying the contents of your drives to your phone or vice versa.

Tip # 34: Swipe to Call or Text

Use your S4 the way it is meant to and swipe to call and text instead of the traditional tapping to perform these actions. How do you go about doing it?

Just go to your contacts, or you can bring the Contacts by asking your device, if you have S Voice enabled. Once in contacts, choose your contact, once again you can just use S voice to get to the contact just by saying 'call 'contact name'' or text 'contact name''. Once you have the contact on your screen, swipe to the left if you want to call the contact, or swipe to the right if you want to text them. If you swipe to the left and decide to text them instead, juts swipe to the right.

Tip # 35: Hidden Settings

You can change some hidden settings that you had no idea you could control using an app called the 'Note 2 Hidden Settings'. This works on all of the Samsung devices so don't fret if you use Samsung S4 not a Note 2. Just go to Play store and download this app. Once installed, open the app and juts follow the instructions provided in the app. You can disable basic built in settings such as sounds, lights etc using this app.

Tip # 36: Get KitKat

TouchWiz is the built in launcher in every Samsung device. It is not a very fun launcher and has a lot of restrictions which can be overcome by downloading another launcher. However you don't have to completely remove the launcher, in order to gain the benefits of another launcher. Just download and run the two to get added benefits. There are a lot of great launchers available in the Google Playstore that can be easily downloaded and run alongside the pre-installed launcher.

Tip # 37: Home Screen

Most Samsung users have no idea that they can fluidly navigate between the Home Screens instead of sliding from one to another and back and forth. On the home screen, there is an indicator which is a series of horizontal white boxes or white tiles which moves when you shift from one home screen to other. If you slide your finger on this indicator, you can choose which screen you want to move to instead of going through one to get to other. You will also see numbers on the screen to show which screen you are on.

Tip # 38: Auto Brightness

One of the biggest problems with a Smartphone is its battery life and similar is the case with the Samsung S4. Even though it is better than most phones, but it still doesn't last long enough. Not surprisingly, the touch screen consumes 50% of the total battery drainage. There is no doubt that the phone sports one of the most gorgeous screens , however what point is a gorgeous screen if the phone won't stay on long enough for us to enjoy using it. It completely beats the purpose of a cell phone.

With this one tip, you can make your battery last longer. In Samsung phones the minimal screen brightness is still bright enough to be sued without having to increase the brightness any further. This is why, in order to save battery use your phone on minimum brightness, which you will discover to your surprise is brilliant on its own. If you use your phone outdoors, keep your screen on auto brightness and your screen will adjust brightness according to the lighting in your surroundings.

Tip # 39: Turn Emails Off

The battery on Smartphones are a big issue, which is why you need these tricks that can combine together to give your battery a huge boost. The second app that is guilty of the highest consumption of battery is the email applications. These applications whether Yahoo, Gmail or Outlook, are set up to constantly sync and check for new emails. To do this, they are constantly connected to internet and automatically loading and reloading. Throughout the day, these apps cause a heavy drain on the battery; no wonder the poor battery doesn't last long enough.

So, you can make your battery last longer by keeping those emails off by signing out of the app every time you exit the app after checking your emails. However if your emails are important and you need to know when you have an email, simply change the frequency of sync for the email app. You can do that by going to the individual settings of each app and selecting sync frequency as once every ten minutes, or five minutes , depending on the urgency of emails.

Tip # 40: Keep an Eye on Your Apps

If your battery is still draining faster than you are using it, you can simply monitor which apps are causing the most drainage by going to the battery monitor. To check the battery monitor, simply go to 'Settings', and select 'battery'. Doing so would guide you to the battery monitor where you can see the percentage battery consumption for each application and monitor what app is draining the most battery.

The biggest advantage of the battery monitor is that you can find out the unnecessary apps that are draining your battery and disable, uninstall or log out of those applications and save a lot of your battery juice.

Tip # 41: Display Time Out

Another fantastic tip for saving battery juice is by checking the screen timeout frequency. Why does this work? Because a lot of times your screen times out long after you have kept the cell down or are done using it. The longer the screen stays on, the longer it is eating away at your battery power.

You can use Smart Stay, which keeps the screen as long as your eye is fixed on it. The moment you move the phone away or put it down, it switches off the display, when it can't see your eyes anymore. If you don't prefer smart stay, the next best option is going to the 'Settings', and selecting 'My display' in this menu, this will open up the display menu.

Under the 'Display' menu, you will find 'Screen Timeout', by selecting this you will be given a menu from which you can select the time out duration, the best option is time out after '30 seconds of inactivity'. This way, it won't switch off when you are still using it, due to the fact that 30 seconds is long enough for you to carry out an activity and still a long enough duration to to switch off the display and save battery, if you don't carry out any activity in that duration.

Tip # 42: *Turn* Wi-Fi Off and *Keep* Bluetooth Off

There are times when all you are worried about is keeping your phone on, when you are down to the last ten or so percent of your battery power. At these times, Bluetooth and Wi-Fi are not a part of your worries; however, by using them wisely they can surely help your case.

Wi-Fi and Bluetooth are right there on the notifications menu to be toggled on and off as per your use. So turn Wi-Fi off and frankly, keep Bluetooth off, no one uses it any longer with the more convenient option of S-Beam available. You will save a whole lot of battery juice by following this tip along with the last two tips.

Tip # 43: Activate Flight Mode

There are a lot of times when you are not even aware of your phone, when you are busy in work, in a meeting, in a class, or driving, perhaps busy doing chores and so on. During these times, it is wiser to save battery because just keeping your device on, is draining your battery due to all those applications running pointlessly on your device. Not to forget the fact, that the battery being used just to keep your phone on.

Instead of switching your phone off, it is wiser to switch it to the 'flight mode', that is why the option is available in the first place. Just by turning the flight mode on, you can switch off all the radios that combined drain your phone battery.

To activate the flight mode, simply go to the notification panel and tap on the airplane icon to enable flight mode and save battery.

Tip # 44: Switch Off Background apps

There is a whole array of fantastically brilliant applications that take the touch screen smart phone experience to a whole new level. Isn't that what the S4 is all about after all? Not, when your sole worry is making your battery last. During these times, it is much more practical to kill the extra applications whose life line is directly linked to your device's battery meter.

To find out what applications are currently running, press and hold the home button. Doing so will take you to a window that shows you a list of currently running apps. Look at the apps and look closely at the buggers draining away at your battery juice. Kill the ones that are not serving you by swiping to the right or left and save your phone.

Tip # 44: Correct Charging Methods

Not a lot of people know how to correctly charge their battery to ensure a long battery life along with making it last longer throughout the day. Any battery will give you better performance if you take good care of its needs. The S4 comes with a 2,600mAh lithium-ion battery and seeks gentle charging in order to perform optimally.

To make your battery last longer, charge it completely, in one go rather than in short bursts. Doing so will improve its daily life and the battery will last longer on the long run, and as a result won't require replacing like most batteries do by the end of a year. Another great tip for extending battery's health is to let the battery drain completely, once a month and then charging it in one go.

Tip # 45: Keep Your Cool

A common complaint with most smart phones is its tendency to overheat frequently. The reason behind this occurrence is the ventilation issue with most Smartphones. The lithium batteries that come with these cell phones don't react well to high temperatures and this causes its performance to deteriorate. To stop this from happening, charge your phone in a well ventilated area and make sure that it is not covered by any cloth, case or any such thing.

Tip # 46: Learn to Use GPS Wisely!

Similar to other radios, GPS is amongst one of the top most battery drainer. You can test this tip out with amazing results. Turn off your GPS, Wi-Fi and Bluetooth at night when turning in for the night. You would be surprised to see barely 5 to 10 percent drainage of battery when you wake up in the morning.

When you're indoors you don't require GPS, or GPRS, so learn to use these radios wisely and make your battery last all day and night long. Also remember to keep the radios off while listening to songs or watching videos to make the most out of your battery life.

Tip # 47: Learn to Speed up Your S4 Launcher

One of the charms of the S4 is its animations. You barely noticed these animations up till now, due to the intended subtleness. These effects are the fading out, fading in and fading from a point and other such effects that smooth the transition from one screen to other. Even though they look good, they make your device's response time slow.

In order to speed up your launcher, you can turn off these animations very simply by going to Samsung Settings menu, going to the 'Developer Options' and uncheck the boxes labeled 'Windows animation scale' as well as 'Transition animation scale'. This will turn off these animations and speed up your cell phone.

Tip # 48: Save Time Changing Ringtones and Alarm Tones

If you are one of those people who carry their playlists with them wherever they go, then you probably have a thousand songs in your cell phone. However this can make changing your ringtone and alarm sounds very tedious due to the fact that all these sounds, songs and tones are stored in one folder, by default. So each time that you want to change your ringtone, you have to go through thousands of audio files to find the one you want to select.

How do you reduce the time each time you want to change your tone? You categorize your tones so that you have separate folders for songs, alarms and ringtones. Doesn't that sound great?

You can categorize your audio files by going to your SD card, using any file manager application downloaded from Playstore. Create a folder labeled as 'Media' in your SD card. Within this folder, create three different folders and label them 'music', 'alarms' and 'ringtones'. Now cut and paste your media files in the right folder amongst the three. For example move all your songs into the folder labeled 'music' and alarms into the correct folder and so on.

Now you will find that when you go to the settings to change your ringtone, you will find three folders instead of the continuous list of mp3s that you were seeing before.

Tip # 49: Learn How to Skip Scanning Unwanted Files

Sometimes you do not want to scan through all the pictures or you don't want all the pictures showing in the gallery. To stop your device from showing a folder in the gallery, just go to the folder and create an empty file with the name .nomedia. The .nomedia file will stop your device from showing the contents of the folder in the gallery.

Tip # 50: Make Sure Your Pictures Look as Good on Computer as they do On Your S4

The screen on S4 is OLED based, which makes colors look brighter than they actually are. On the one hand, this makes using the Smartphone an amazing experience, but it also goofs up the picture colors. How does it do that? It makes the pictures look brighter than they really are, and when you transfer these files to the computer to upload on any social media platform, you will find that these pictures look very dull in comparison with what they looked like on the phone.

The solution? Go to the settings menu and select the Display options. In the Display options, choose the screen settings 'natural' to make sure the pictures appear as what they naturally are.

Tip # 51: Play All Media Formats

Many Smartphone users like to carry episodes of their favorite TV series and other video files in their phone to watch in their spare time, on the move. However Samsung S4 users might be disappointed to know that the video player that comes pre installed with Samsung S4, doesn't support a lot of formats such as mkv, which is pretty popular these days.

The solution? Download other better players from Google Playstore and play all your favorite videos in any format easily. VLC player is one of the best players these days. Simply go to Playstore, search fro VLC player, and download the app.

Once installed, open the player and you will find all the videos in your device, displayed right there in the player. Select any video and enjoy.

Tip # 51: Multi Task While Watching Videos

There are a lot of times when we are watching videos, we feel like getting information on actors or other movies and references. To do this, we have to end the movie, open browser and then carry out the search. However with the S4, you can multitask while watching videos. Isn't that amazing?

You can do this by opening the video player and then tapping on the little icon on the bottom right corner that has an icon of two screens, one smaller screen on top of a smaller screen. You will instantly see the screen reduce in size and your home screen will appear below it, allowing you to carry out any tasks you like.

Tip # 52: Play Free Games

Possibly one of the best uses of Samsung S4's beautiful screen is playing free games on it. Try a 3D game to take the gaming experience to the next level. You can find a wide variety of free games on Google Playstore under the tab free applications.

Tip # 53: Control Screen Brightness

If you have set your screen brightness on auto, and you want to increase the brightness when outside or while watching videos, you might want to switch off the auto brightness and manually control the screen brightness. You can do so by going to the notifications pane and using the screen brightness control to adjust it according to your preference.

Tip # 54: Output Video from Your S4 to Your TV Screens

We have all used HDMI cables to output our laptops' displays on bigger screens to enhance our video watching experience. However it is not convenient to carry our laptops everywhere with us. Now there is an alternative solution for S4 users. This feature increases the brilliance of Samsung S4 and takes it to a whole new level. You can connect your device to an external cable to output the display to a larger screen such as a TV screen or your laptop etc. In fact it can output not only the video, but its amazing surround sound audio. This cable fits into the microUSB port and has an HDMI convertor on the other end, which easily fits into your big screens. Now enjoy your videos anywhere with your device.

Tip # 55: Watch Movies with Surround Sound

If you are watching videos on your S4, you might want to enhance the experience using the Surround Sound option that the S4 comes with. In order to do this, you need to enable surround sound by going to the Settings menu, and checking the box labeled 'Surround Sound'. If you want to output surround sound, make sure you tick the Surround box within the Accessory menu in the Settings menu.

Tip # 56: Add Cool Widgets

Even though there is a nice selection of widgets to choose from in the ones provided by Samsung, however one can never have enough widgets and it's always fun to try new fun widgets. You can try these fun widgets as well for your home screen when you get tired of the same old widgets. Just go to the Google Playstore and search for widgets. You will find amazing widget packages that will add class, funk or whatever is that you are looking for; you are bound to find something to match your preferences.

Tip # 57: Tilt Control Your Phone

Control your phone and command it to do whatever you want, just by tilting it. You can enable the tilt control by going to the settings menu and selecting the tilt control option.

Tip # 58: Go Sci-Fi with your S4

Now you can get your Samsung to unlock your phone by scanning your face. Isn't that brilliant! Now there is no need of pass codes and patterns, with this amazing feature, only you have access to your phone. It works by taking a picture of your face and then scanning your face and matching that with the picture in its memory. If it matches, you gain access to your phone. It is an impressive feature alright!

Tip # 59: Get Surrounded With Jelly Beans

One of the most entertaining hidden tricks on a Samsung device is the jelly bean trick. It is as simple as 123, yet not many people know about it. Just go to settings menu and go to the 'About device section'. Many people cannot get this trick right even though they know about it, due to the fact that there is a special way you must tap the menu to bring about the jelly beans.

Tap continuously on the 'Android version number', even though it's not highlighted nor does anything, jut bear with us and continue tapping. In no time, you will see a giant jelly bean on your screen. Now here is the best part, if you continue tapping the giant jelly bean, you will find your screen filling up with jelly beans which you can play and flick around to your heart's content and delight.

Tip # 60: Categorize Your Music

Now you can listen to songs that match your mood, or the exact opposite if you are distressed and would like to listen to something upbeat. Your Samsung S4 allows you to arrange the music in your device according to your mood. There is a small 5 by 5 square in the pre-installed music player that has a little extra feature called the Music square. This music square has tiny boxes that represent different moods and will categorize your song list according to the different moods. By tapping on any of the moods, your device will play songs according to the mood you selected.

Tip # 62: Get Yourself Some Extra Memory

Even though the Samsung Smartphones come with substantial internal memories, however one can never have enough memory can they? To make yourself some extra space, make sure to keep your cache and temporary files folder clean.

To do so, go to the settings, and into the application manager. In the application manager, you will see a long list of applications. Tap each application and you will be taken to a page where you will be given the option to clear cache, go on clearing cache of each application.

Tip # 63: HDR Camera Mode

The camera on the Samsung S4 is one of the best cameras on Smartphones, however there are a few tips and tricks that can enhance your pictures taking them to the next level. You must play around with the different modes to get the most out of your device; it has some of the most fabulous modes ever. The HDR mode that comes with the amazing camera app, in a S4 is a must try for taking fabulous pictures. This little feature adds extra details to one picture by taking multi angled shot and combining into one picture. When you take a shot with the HDR mode, you are also saving your pictures in the normal mode so that you can select which ever picture you like more in the two. It is a win for everyone.

Tip # 64: Motion Modes

How many times have we wanted to get a series of shots without having to continuously and repeatedly pressing the capture button to take individual shots? Now the Samsung S4 comes with a solution for this little problem as well, it is in the form of motion modes which capture a series of shots at once.

To select the slow or fast motion modes, go into the menu of the camera where you will find these modes and selecting them will allow you to take either more pictures or less than normal, depending on which mode you select.

Tip # 65: Awesome Video Effects

We all love the result of the pictures taken from a professional camera, however very few of us can afford it, especially after indulging on an S4. However here is the best part, your S4 comes with some amazing effects that are very close to those that can be carried out using a professional camera. There are a wide variety of exciting filters that enhance the results of videos and pictures taken from the device, such as the color pop which drains all colors from the picture except any one or two colors that you choose, or the cartoon filter which will make any scene you snap, into a page out of a comic book.

Tip # 66: Hold Longer For Better Pictures

To our amazement, there are many times that the view looks great on the screen of the camera, before you capture it, but not so great after we actually look at the picture after capturing it. What brings out the difference in the pre capture view and after it has been captured?

We have discovered that one small trick can make a world of difference in your pictures. When you press the capture button for capturing the pictures, do not immediately let go of the capture button after hearing the shutter sound. Instead of immediately letting go, hold on to the capture button for a moment or two longer, because our device doesn't immediately capture the shot after pressing the button and hearing the shutter sound but rather a second or two after it. So give your device the time by holding on to the capture button for two seconds more.

Tip # 67: Preview Videos

Has it ever happened that you stopped watching a clip or a video and had to scroll through the whole video to find where you stopped it?

Well, Samsung S4 comes with a solution to this problem as well, with the air view which allows you to preview videos using a little window that opens up showing you what scene you will find at what time in the video. All you have to do is move your finger over the transport bar which shows where you are currently in the video. By hovering at multiple places around the bar you can find the spot where you stopped watching the video.

Tip # 68: Sound Settings

The factory settings of the Samsung S4 are by default, very loud. Many people don't like their cell phones all that loud, which is why you might want to play with the settings in order to bring all the sounds up or down to your preference. You will find most of the sound settings in the settings menu, while a few of them need to be tweaked by going to individual app settings. To do so, go into the settings and in to the sound menu, you might want to uncheck or keep checked, some of the options available according to your preference.

You have the option to mute the dialing sounds, the typing sounds, sounds for the notification alerts, touch sounds and many such beeps and sounds that can be quite irritating for someone constantly using their phone and for the people present in the same room, as well.

Tip # 69: Fast Settings

Every little feature in the S4 is about convenience of the user. This is why you do not have to go all the way into the settings to find the most used settings. For this purpose a set of settings known as the fast settings are available and can be accessed by going into the notification panel and dragging the notification shade down, using not one, but two fingers. This brings up four rows of those settings that are most frequently used. From this menu, you can tap and activate any of the settings you require such as GPRS, Wi-Fi, Sound, Airplane Mode, Screen Rotation, and many other such settings.

Tip # 70: Smart Switch

If you are switching from an iPhone or a BlackBerry to your S4, you might want to carry all your contacts, files, media and what not, to your new device. This can never be an easy feat; however Samsung gives you an easier option for making the switch using Samsung's computer application. This application known as the 'Smart Switch' can very easily transfer all your data from your old device to your S4 by creating a backup in iTunes.

Tip # 70: Block Stalkers

Life can be hard when you come out of a difficult relationship; however it can get even more challenging if your ex keeps calling you. To make it easier to get over old relationships, use the call blocking app and block all the numbers that you never want to receive a call from, ever.

Just go to the 'My Settings' menu and into 'My device' menu. Select 'Call' options in the menu you see in front of you. Inside the 'Call options' you will see an option labeled as "Call Block', by clicking on this you can enter any number you want to block and save it. Voila! You will never receive another call from them again as long as you are using this phone.

Tip # 71: Delete Unwanted Apps

Many people go wild when they start installing apps, to the degree that they install hundreds of apps that they rarely ever use. After a few months, or weeks, you don't even remember why you installed the app at that time. Instead of cluttering your device, keep your S4 clean by regularly deleting and getting rid of old and unused apps that are causing a strain on your phone's RAM, and memory as well.

Simply go to 'My Settings' menu and tap the 'More' option amongst the tabs given in the settings menu. Select 'Application Manager' and you will see a long list of all the apps that you have installed on your device. Select the one you want to delete and tap it, this will take you to app settings, which also has the option to uninstall the app. Click this touch button to uninstall the app, go on uninstalling the apps you don't want from the previous list.

Tip # 72: Update to the Latest Software

There are people who like to keep up to date with all the new software releases and the latest tech innovations. If you are one of those people, and love new releases due to all the updated features and interesting tips and tricks that are incorporated into these new OS updates. You can easily update your S4 software even if your device doesn't give you the option or if you don't like waiting till your device gives you the option to update.

Simply go to settings menu and tap the 'More' option amongst the tabs given in the settings menu. In the options in front of you, select the 'About device' section and tap the Software Update option given there. When the device asks you to update, click on 'update' and you will find your device being updated.

Tip # 73: Get the Best Browser Experience

Google Chrome is single handedly one of the best browsers on Android and off. Although S4 doesn't come with pre-installed Google chrome, you might want to install the browser and enjoy a smooth browsing experience that comes with it.

Simply go to the Google Playstore and search for "Google Chrome', you will find the search display a lot of browsers but find the "Google Chrome' amongst the search results and tap on it. This will take you to the app and give you the option to install it. Go ahead, install and enjoy!!

Tip # 74: Organize Your Media

Samsung S4 is an awesome phone; however its picture gallery is not all that fun. It's cluttered and makes viewing pictures pretty complicated, which is why installing an external application for your picture gallery is a better option. Flayvr is an excellent app that can be easily found in the Google Playstore. In order to install the app, start by searching for the app in the Playstore search bar and going to the app once you spot it, by tapping on the search result. Go into the app and install it. Once installed, open it and follow the directions of the app to organize and merge all your media in one app.

Automatically all your media will be sorted by time, making it easier to find files when you are looking for them.

Tip # 75: Enjoy Free Game: Angry Birds Star Wars II

One of the most entertaining features of an S4, is its huge screen and HD graphics. Combine that with the surround sound quality and you have got yourself a mini gaming station. One of the best ways of passing time whenever you are bored is by playing games on your S4. In the coming pages, we will introduce you to a few of the most popular games, which will have you hooked and playing for hours at end.

One such game is the Angry Birds Star Wars II, which is available completely free of cost in the Google Playstore. The craze for the adorable angry birds has taken a new face with this star wars themed game. Even though the theme and scenarios are different, the game is as fun as the previous versions. This is why the addiction is striking people of all age.

Enjoy playing as Darth Maul, Darth Vader, Emperor, Mace Windu, General Grievous, Yoda, Anakin, Jango Fett and many such characters from the original star wars themed angry birds. If you are a Star Wars lover and an Angry Birds lover, you will love this game without doubt.

Tip # 76: Get Professional

An S4 is not all about entertainment; however it is about ease and convenience. With Samsung S4, keeping up with office work is easier than ever. However in order to utilize your Smartphone for professional work, you require an app that is as professional as you. The Officesuite Professional 7 is just that app.

In order to install the app, start by searching for the app in the Playstore search bar and going to the app once you spot it by tapping on the search result. Go into the app and install it. Once installed, open it and follow the directions of the app.

This brilliant app allows you to open, read and edit your office documents at home or out, wherever you are. Do you have a long commute to and back from work? If, yes then this is an excellent time for preparing for presentations or any other office tasks that you didn't get time to go through, the day before. This app makes it really convenient to get work done whenever you have spare time, and it eliminates the need to lug around your laptop all day, wherever you go.

Tip # 77: Make the Most Out of Your Smartphone Using Skype

One of the most utilized features of a Smartphone is its ability to make video calls completely free of cost. When it comes to video conferences, can there be any app better than Skype? This is one smart app that can allow you to make calls any time of the day to anyone, using your S4. All you require is a good internet connection, which is available almost everywhere these days, making this a must have app.

Once again, in order to install the app, you have to start by searching for the app in the Playstore, using the search bar. Once you spot the app, tap it to go into the app description page. Once you are in the description page, click on the 'install app' button.

.

Tip # 78: Connect to a Professional Network

Are you looking for a good career opportunity? Or are you someone who is responsible for the hiring in your company or perhaps you just like a good professional network that has qualified and knowledgeable people. Whatever it may be, you would love having a presence on Linked in; it is an ideal resource for finding jobs, connecting to professional people from all over the world. This app is a must have for people looking for jobs, because if you have an attractive resume, you will come across companies who are looking for individuals like you right there on Linked In and it pays to have a good connection here.

Go to your menu and locate Playstore, click on the app to open it. Once Playstore is open, you can spot a search bar right there on the homepage. Search for LinkedIn and once you spot the app, tap it to go into the app description page. Once you are in the description page, click on the 'install app' button.

After installing the app, you will be required to create an account and enter all details related to your career and education background. When that's done, you can start by looking for people you know and then simply connect with other people through your friends.

Tip # 79: Make Your Mornings Better

There are many people who can achieve so much if only they could get to their appointments on time, which requires waking up early in the morning. Make your S4, your key to success using an application that will make waking up in the morning as easy as 123. This app is known as Alarm clock plus and can be found in the Playstore.

Alarm Clock Plus is a very smart little application that is very easy to manage and operate. Just go to the settings of the application, once you have it installed, you can customize the application according to your preferences that makes waking up early in the morning easy. Record your voice to play as the alarm sound in the morning, or set ten alarms at a ten minutes interval each, to make sure that you wake up or keep a snooze sound that you won't be able to sleep through. This app let's you do all that and more.

Tip # 80: Access Your Computer Wherever You Are

You are already on your way and you realize you forgot to get a file from your computer and now you have to go back to your office or your home to get the file. There is a better solution to incidents like these. Using your S4, you can easily access your files wherever you are from your desktop.

This is possible using an application known as "Remote Desktop HD". Using this app, you can bring any file on your computer to your device as easy as 123. You can get any excel, word or PowerPoint file, using this application. In order to install this application, go to Playstore in your device's menu and open Playstore.

Search for this app in Playstore and install it. Once installed, open the app and follow the directions given on the app, you will have to install n app on your computer as well, to connect it with your device.

Tip # 81: Send and receive Compressed Files

If you work on heavy files at work, or would like to send any large media files such as picture folder or videos, you can easily do it with your S4. This is not an easy task, any Smartphone user understands the difficulty that transferring huge files can be. However you can simply compress the file and email it to anyone using the Androzip File Manager. This application can also be found on the Playstore. Simply by searching for it and downloading it, you can avail the twofold benefits of this application.

Not only a file compressor, this application is also an awesome file manager using which you can manage all your files easily such as transferring files, moving, copying them or transferring them from or to a computer. You can also unzip and extract compressed file sent by others.

Tip # 82: Any. Do

Your S4 can be an ultimate tool if it is utilized completely. Manage your schedules and appointments with your S4, just by speaking into it. You can set your appointments, make notes, record your thoughts by talking out loud into your phone and it will record all of it for you to refer back, whenever you desire. Not only that, you can sync your schedule so that your friends can easily access it, or send it to your friends so they know when you are available or what time you have to meet them and so on.

Tip # 83: Protect Your Device

If your S4 has to become your ultimate tool and support system, you need to protect it to ensure it lasts long because the last thing you want is your device to get infected and not function up to the par. You can easily protect and keep your device virus free by installing 'Bitdefender Antivirus' via the Google Playstore. This is another amazing free application, which will protect your device from any cyber threat and make sure it remains efficient for longer.

Another great feature of this application is that it will not eat into your battery like other antivirus on the market. It will also not slow your device down, and instead keep it working smoothly.

Tip #84: Keep Your Smartphone Smart

Do you find your faithful S4 lagging and slowing down? Well if so, then you need to install an application that will clean up your phone to bring its performance back up to the optimum level. One such application is known as the 'Clean Master'.

It can carry out several functions to keep your S4 running as smoothly as ever.

Clean up Internet Cache and Temporary Folders

With ten and hundreds of applications on your device, you wouldn't even know which application is making your device slow down. These files can build up and occupy a large chunk of your S4's memory. However, the clean master, will make sure that no such files get to stay in your device by deleting them as soon as they build up.

Correct the Speed of Your Device

When unnecessary applications run in the background, your device will slow down. Even if you keep on killing these applications, they have been programmed to restart after a set interval. As a result, you can never really kill these apps but they will slow your device down if you let them have their way. However, using Clean Master, you can save your RAM and make your battery last longer, as it will stop any such application from restarting and running in the background.

Tip # 85: Use your Device in the Dark

If you find yourself stranded out on the road because your car broke down, or you want to look for something in the dark, or in any such situation, you can easily turn your S4 into a smart flashlight which can come to your aid in the worst of times.

Simply go to Google store and download an application known as 'flashlight'. Once you have the application installed, open it and go ahead shine your device in any dark corners or down any dark alleys, or simply to look for something during the night, when you just don't feel like getting up to switch on the light.

Tip # 86: Stream Songs

Everyone loves listening to non-stop music, while working, driving, shopping, exercising and so on. Any activity can become interesting with good music playing in the background. However, it can get tedious to download new songs and change your playlist every few days, especially when you are short on time. Your best bet, in such times is to listen to music online. But listening to music online can get tedious as well, if you have to search and locate your favorite songs every day.

This is why android users prefer listening to their favorite tracks on Spotify. It is one of the best music applications due to its vast library of old and new songs which you can stream and listen non-stop wherever you are. Easily create a playlist by tapping on your favorite songs, or listen to one of the mood based playlists on Spotify. You can find Spotify and download it via the Google Playstore.

Tip # 87: Keep an Eye on the Weather

Don't get stuck in bad weather, when you could very easily plan ahead for it, making sure that you can be in the right place at the right time. After all, every spare moment is precious when you could spend it engaged in one of your favorite activities instead of out on the road or in the office etc, waiting for the weather to calm down.

Your solution for bad weather is, the 1Weather app, which is one of the most installed and maximum rated apps in the Google Play Store. Get your weather alerts and forecasts in real time, making sure you are always prepared for the weather. You can get minute by minute or hourly weather alerts, whether in office or on the move.

Tip # 88: Share Your Pictures

It is not possible that an android user has not heard of Instagram and the total picture sharing pleasure that this app is. Stay up to date with what your friends are doing, through the pictures they are uploading or pictures that others in your location are uploading. This is one of the greatest and easiest ways of finding out what some of the greatest places to hangout are, or what some of the best places to eat are, and where everyone is at the moment etc.

On top of that, you can share your own experiences with your friends by uploading these pictures on Instagram wherever you are, so that you can laugh and discuss the moment even after it is over. It is very easy to use and you can also set your device to automatically sync all your pictures to Instagram. However make sure to turn the sync option off, if you don't want the whole world to see all of your pictures on their homepage.

Tip # 89: Organize and Backup your Phone

Evernote is by far one of the easiest ways of organizing your S4. You can very simply add all your planning tools in this one app, such as your notes, screenshots, to do task lists and so on. It gives you the option to create to do lists, create and edit notes, as well as making task lists. One of the truly great features of this app is that it has an audio recording feature that allows you to create notes by speaking into the device. This is a feature that makes note making so convenient now that you no longer have to locate a pen for making notes and you can go back to the app and hear what notes you made.

It also allows you to upload pictures so that you may want to snap the picture of event invitations, movies you want to rent, things you want to buy or simply passwords that you cannot remember, and so on. You can access these notes from your S4 or any other device no matter where in the world you are, which makes accessing and organizing so simple that you would become addicted to this amazing app.

Tip # 90: Color Sheep

Another great game that is available free of cost on the Google Playstore is Color Sheep. This is an incredibly exciting game that tests the sharpness and speed of minds. It is not very difficult to understand, but it requires a perplexing arrangement of moves in order to ace the game. In order to win, you have to save the sheep on your screen, from getting devoured by wolves.

In order to save these sheep, you have to change the color of their wool coat, to the same color of the wolf's coat, which are gradually gaining on your sheep. That sounds pretty simple, right? Don't be so sure. Changing the color of the sheep's coat is not as simple as you might be thinking. In order to swap the wool color of the sheep in distress, you are required to match the shade on the wolf's coat by mixing the three primary colors, red, blue and green, in just the right quantities to create the exact same color on the wolf's coat.

However, the difficulty of the task doesn't end there. Once you have matched the color of the sheep's coat with that of the wolf's fur, you are required to lighten or darken the color to match the exact same shade of the wolf's fur with that of the sheep. Now isn't that an exciting game!

Tip # 91: Candy Crush

Candy Crush is one of those free games that is not only addicting, challenging but is so delicious that you would find it very hard to resist the sweet addiction this game will prove to be. It begins as an easy game but gets progressively harder. Surprisingly the harder it gets, the more addicting this game becomes. If you fail to complete a game in the available tries, you will lose a life.

If you lose all the lives, you would have to wait for an extra half hour to accumulate all the lives again, before you can continue playing. Even though this doesn't feel like much of a penalty, you will feel the harshness of the half hour when you are so hooked to the game that the half hour would feel like an impossibly long duration of time. This is a must try game because you can update and compete with your friends on Facebook or anyone in the world for that matter. This makes the game even more fun due to the challenge of beating your friend's scores and exceeding their scores.

Tip # 92: Temple Run 2

If Temple Run wasn't enough of a success and addiction, the creators have released a sequel to the game which is even more challenging and addicting. What fun is a game that isn't addicting right? Well Temple Run 2 has everything that makes a game, addicting. It has brilliant graphics, along with intricate details, that together combine to make the game almost real like, with sound effects that make your heart pound.

Along with improved graphics, the challenges have improved as well compared to Temple Run 1. You have now a wider array of life like obstacles you need to cross in order to escape the monster. These obstacles include waterfalls, wheel barrow, rivers, and so on. This not only increases the difficulty levels, but makes the game that much more enjoyable and entertaining.

Tip # 93: CSR Racing

Racing games are a legend amongst games, with a genre of their own. The adrenaline rush that comes with playing a racing game beats everything else. This game is an ideal game for someone who is interested in cars due to the fact that you can customize and create your own car before racing it. Now isn't that exciting! You can also race with your friends because this is a multiplayer game, which increases the fun factor by ten times. This game is very detail oriented and the graphics are brilliant, which is part of the reason of what makes this game an intensely entertaining game.

Tip # 94: Despicable Me 2

The minions rage has affected people all around the globe, but that is not surprising at all due to the fact that these little creatures are possibly the most adorable of all animated characters. Their mischievousness and love for bananas is well captured in this version of the game. The graphics and sound effects resemble those found in the movie as well as all the other characters in the movie.

This game contains scenes and comics that will make you roll over with laughter, loving every moment of the game unable to set it down. This is the perfect way to relax at the end of a tiring day. This game is not only for kids but for adults as well who can understand the details and grasp the full meaning of the jokes included in the game.

Even though the game is entertaining, and funny, it is not an easy game as it is filled with loads of challenges and difficulties, as well as trying to get the minion to do what you ask him to do. Overall, this is one adorable must play game for everyone.

Tip # 95: Butcher House

Enjoy reading but never have enough time to sit down with a good book? If you crave reading and getting so engrossed into a book that it feels like you are in a trance, unable to tear yourself away from the book, this is the perfect solution for you. Did you know that your S4 can become your favorite book as well? There are a wide variety of free eBooks available online on the internet that you can easily download and read on your device. You can also download one of the many free eBooks apps that are available on the Google Playstore, just by searching for 'free eBooks', on the Playstore, you will find hundreds of free books.

One of our favorite apps for free eBooks is 'Butcher House'. As the name suggests, it is a horror story app. Who doesn't love reading a good chilling book? This app has 700 of the scariest horror stories ranging from gore to ghosts, vampires to demons and whatnot!

The best part is that you can carry your book everywhere with you in your device without any added weight which comes with a paperback book. Read anywhere you find yourself with a few spare moments.

Tip # 96: Classical Guitar

Are you one of those people who have always wanted to learn how to play a guitar but never got down to it due to any reason whatsoever! Well, now you have the means to learn playing guitar in your hands! Your device can become your teacher by simply downloading an app that will teach you to play guitar by taking you through all the basics and advanced tips, tricks and details.

This app is so life like, that you won't feel like you are playing a virtual guitar but an actual one. It vibrates when you strum the strings giving it a very real like feel. It even accommodates left handed guitar players! Begin with this app and in no time, you will be a master guitar player using the real instrument.

Tip # 97: Minecraft – Pocket Edition

One of the games that is all the rage these days is Minecraft. This game allows you to get creative by building stuff that you can use in the game like buildings, mines, tables, holes, armor, houses and even castles. The best part is that in order to get creative, you require a whole list of raw material that you acquire while playing this game. These raw materials include stones, bricks, blocks, mud and a whole list of such buildable items, while keeping yourself safe from deadly mobs. This is one adventurous and addictive game that had got people from all around the hooked. One of the best uses of your device is by playing this game.

Tip # 98: PBS Video

Many people like to use their S4 to catch up on old reruns of their favorite shows or the latest episodes of their current favorite show. By downloading PBS, you can watch a whole list of your favorite shows by streaming them on this app. On top of that, you can share your favorite shows with your friends on social media to share with them your current favorite TV series. So, enjoy unlimited entertainment, watching episodes of any TV show wherever you are.

Tip # 99: Pinterest

One of the most resourceful apps of today is Pinterest, it has information on everything that might interest you. There is hardly anything that is not available here. It is an online pin board for all that interests everyone on earth such as fitness information, healthy recipes, motivating quotes, gossip, DIYs, trip ideas, and whatnot. You can share the information you find interesting online with your friends and the entire world by opining it here. Simply download Pinterest on Google Playstore and start exploring.

Tip # 100: Pocket

Do you like browsing on your S4? Why wouldn't you! It has the smoothest, most exciting screen amongst all Smartphones. However one of the problems of browsing on your phone is that you can't save the articles you read, unless you want to take a snapshot. However with this application you can store anything you find interesting online in one place, in the form of a notebook. Isn't that wonderful!

Simply download this application on your device using the Google Playstore and start adding content to the pocketbook, so that you can very conveniently refer back to this app whenever you want to share an article with someone or refer back to what you read , or collect recipes, tips, tricks in one place.